THOMAS A[RNE]

(1710–1778)

8 Keyboard Sonatas

8 Sonaten für Tasteninstrumente
8 Sonates pour Clavier

Edited by
Herausgegeben von : Editées par

CHRISTOPHER HOGWOOD

FABER *ff* MUSIC

© 1983 by Faber Music Ltd
First published in 1983 by Faber Music Ltd
Bloomsbury House 74–77 Great Russell Street London WC1B 3DA
Music engraved by Jack Thompson
Cover design by Shirley Tucker
Printed in England by Caligraving Ltd
All rights reserved

ISBN10: 0-571-50703-4
EAN13: 978-0-571-50703-0

To buy Faber Music publications or to find out about the full range of titles available
please contact your local retailer or Faber Music sales enquiries:

Faber Music Limited, Burnt Mill, Elizabeth Way, Harlow, CM20 2HX England
Tel: +44 (0) 1279 82 89 82   Fax: +44 (0) 1279 82 89 83
sales@fabermusic.com   fabermusic.com

Contents : Inhalt : Table

INTRODUCTION

John Stafford Smith, who knew Arne well, once described him as 'a conceited Papist, an evil-living man, but a God-gifted genius for melody', and it was undoubtedly his lyrical talent that compensated for the irregularities of his life and character. He was born in the year of Handel's arrival in England (1710), and when he died in 1778, Mozart was already 22 and about to write his 'Paris' symphony. Like so many of the composers of this unsettled but adventurous period, Arne found English music in transition from the established Handelian manner to the lighter, more 'affected' style of the early classical writers; the suite was giving way to the sonata, minuets and gavottes were preferred to preludes and fugues.

Arne's career lay primarily in the theatre, where his melodic gifts ensured his success not only in Italianate opera, but in masque and pantomime as well. His appointment in 1754 as composer to the Vauxhall Gardens meant that, in addition to songs, he was also required to produce organ concertos which were a feature of the concerts there. Apart from this, his published output of concerted instrumental music consisted of orchestral overtures and a set of seven trio sonatas.

Possibly because he was a Catholic (unlike any of his well-known musical contemporaries) Arne left no organ voluntaries, and in fact his only published works for solo keyboard were the sonatas announced by John Walsh in the *Public Advertizer* for November 26, 1756:

NEW MUSIC
This day is published, Price 6s.
EIGHT Sonatas or Lessons for the
Harpsichord, compos'd by Mr. Arne

The collection shows every sign of having been put together hastily. It was unusual to have eight sonatas in a set (rather than six or twelve), and the sequence of movements and keys in several sonatas is particularly haphazard, suggesting that they were assembled from a number of random movements. In some places Arne himself has suggested a short linking passage to smooth an awkward transition (as in Sonata 1), but in other places it has to be supplied by the player (Sonatas 2 and 6).

From the other composers advertised by Walsh on Arne's original title-page (Galuppi, Ciampi, Alberti, Pasquini, Bononcini, etc.) the Italian bias of English taste can readily be deduced. Arne was particularly adventurous amongst the English in following the innovations of Zipoli, Alberti, and, most obviously, Scarlatti. He was one of the 'several Subscribers' (along with Avison, Boyce, Pepusch, Stanley and Geminiani) to the two-volume set of Scarlatti's sonatas that appeared in 1739, and the influence shows clearly in the *allegro* movements of Sonatas 1 and 3, as well as in the final variation of Sonata 6. However, the shorter and more nervous phrases of the opening of Sonata 2 reflect the *galant* manner of the German writers, and the following Adagio (a curiously detached movement that needs some explanation) is the nearest that Arne ever approached to the English voluntary.

Sonata 3 opens with a Prelude, to which Arne adds the instructions that 'In this and other Preludes, which are meant as Extempore Touches before the Lesson begins, neither the Composer nor the Performer are oblig'd to a Strictness of Time'. Handel had included several such preludes in his first collection of keyboard suites, and the whole of this sonata aims at a weightier, more baroque effect than the previous two, with definite 'solo' and 'tutti' passages in the second movement that reflect the concerto grosso.

The longest and most heterogeneous sonata (No. 4) offers most evidence of the disparate elements that Arne drew upon to make up the set. Both the splendidly off-beat fugue (the only fugue in the collection) and the final 'jigg' are forthright examples of the English style, written in a way that is perfectly idiomatic to the keyboard. The opening Andante, equally idiomatic, leans more towards the 'expressive' manner, with much use of the 'sighing-cadence' and some very cunningly extended passages of syncopated chromaticism; the Siciliano, however, lies so uneasily on the keyboard that it can more easily be seen as a hasty adaptation of a movement originally for a melody instrument and figured bass.[1]

Arne himself admitted to the casual origins of Sonata 8 in his inscription: 'The following Plain Minuet is not Mr. Arne's; but (at the request of a Lady) he compos'd the Bass, and Variations that follow, in Order to make it an agreeable Lesson for the Harpsichord'. The same melody (with slight extensions) was later borrowed by Tenducci as an aria in his Pasticcio *Athridates* (published by John Johnston in 1767), where it was sung to the words 'Where is pitty's melting Eye?' and attributed to 'Mr. Rameau'.[2]

Since no autograph of the sonatas has survived, the present edition is based on the 1756 Walsh publication (source **A** in the Editorial Notes); oblong folio, paginated 2-32. The title-page reads: VIII / SONATAS / OR / LESSONS FOR THE HARPSICHORD / COMPOS'D BY / THOMAS AUGUSTINE ARNE./ [rule] / London. Printed for I. Walsh in Catharine Street in the Strand. / [extended advertisement].

Judging from the number of surviving copies in European and American collections, this publication would seem to have been a popular success, but the sonatas were not reissued until 1879, when Ernst Pauer included them (with substantial editorial additions) in his enterprising volume of *Old English Composers for the Virginals & Harpsichord* (London, Augener & Co.). In 1969 a 'facsimile reproduction of the first edition' was issued (Stainer & Bell Ltd, London), based on a copy of the 1756 publication then belonging to Thurston Dart, and now in the library of the Music Department, King's College, London University. This copy is, unfortunately, something of a 'rogue' example. A small number of emendations to the text (mostly the removal of left-hand trills)

---

1. Further discussion of the historical position of Arne's sonatas can be found in 'Arne and the keyboard sonata' by A. E. F. Dickinson, *The Monthly Musical Record*, May 1955, pp. 88-95, and *The Sonata in the Baroque Era*, pp. 328-330, William S. Newman, The University of North Carolina Press, 1959.
2. Information kindly supplied by John A. Parkinson.

suggest a second issue of the first edition, although no other example has so far been noted. It also contains substantial MS additions, in what is said to be an 18th-century hand; they include ties, slurs, 'V.S.' indications for page turns, 'directs', and (for the 18th century) an astonishing number of cautionary and redundant accidentals.[3] The fact that the original print was (in its own terms) surprisingly free from misprints and omissions argues against the MS additions being oversights of the composer, and since no connection with Arne can be established, readings from this source are indicated as editorial or listed in the Editorial notes as source **B**.

The present edition is therefore the first modern printing to represent the standard text of 1756. Editorial additions are shown by the use of square brackets [ ], small notes, rests and accidentals, and ⌐───⌐ . A single passage notated in the tenor clef (Sonata 4, movement 3, bb. 10-12) has been modernized, but the original inconsistencies of triplet notation (in Sonata 2, for instance, almost never with a slur, and Sonata 7 almost always) have been retained. Indications of right and left hand allocation have been preserved, together with the figured bass supplied to the theme of Sonata 8 (which can easily be realized by reference to the following variations). Arne's short linking cadenzas and *arpeggio* sections (a basis for simple improvised flourishes) provide succinct models that players might use elsewhere (in Sonatas 2 and 6 for example).

There are few rhythmic problems in Arne's notation; Sonata 4 and Sonata 7 provide examples of compound metre notated in simple form, and note values must be assimilated to 6/8 and 12/8 respectively. Similarly, Arne's use of ornaments is sparing and lucid; *tr* and ⁕ (trill and lower mordent) are his only abbreviations. (The single appearance of ⁕ in Sonata 4, movement 1, bar 25 is obviously an engraving error for ⁕ .) Trills almost always require a termination, whether indicated or not, and

---

[3] In the facsimile edition these additions are unfortunately indistinguishable from the engraved text.

generally begin on the upper note. However, short trills beginning on the principal note are recognized by many authors after about 1750, but only in certain contexts. Writers such as J. C. Heck, Edward Miller and James Hook illustrate them 'only used in descending Notes' e.g.

(c.f. Sonata 2, movement 3 and Sonata 7, movement 3). An appoggiatura ♩♩ is very often to be interpreted with a trill on the second note, and the cadence figure ♩. ♪♩♩ invariably with a trill on the first. The appoggiatura itself (usually but not always notated by Arne as half the value of the note to which it is attached) 'should be made pretty long, giving it more than half the Length or Time of the Note it belongs to' (Geminiani, 1751). Exceptions, which might be regarded as on-beat or before-the-beat acciaccaturas, include fast-moving passages and triplet figures such as [music example] where, according to C. P. E. Bach 'the appoggiatura must be played quickly, so that the rhythm remains clear and distinguishable from [music example] .'

Arne's use of ♩♪♩ in the Andante of Sonata 4 (the most 'empfindsam' of the set) is clearly an alternative to C. P. E. Bach's ∾ .

I am grateful to the following libraries for their co-operation in the preparation of this edition:

University of London, King's College
British Library, Reference Division
Rowe Music Library, King's College, Cambridge
Royal College of Music
University of London, Music Library
Reid Music Library of the University of Edinburgh

and to Dr. Howard Ferguson for his scrupulous assistance.

© Christopher Hogwood
Cambridge 1982

v

EINFÜHRUNG

John Stafford Smith, der Arne gut kannte, beschrieb ihn einmal als "einen selbstgefälligen Papisten, einen Mann mit frevelhaftem Lebenswandel, aber ein gottbegnadetes Genie für die Melodie", und zweifellos war es sein lyrisches Talent, das für die Unregelmäßigkeiten seines Lebens und seines Charakters entschädigte. Er war in dem Jahr von Händels Ankunft in England (1710) geboren, und als er 1778 starb, war Mozart bereits 22 Jahre alt und im Begriff seine Pariser Sinfonie zu schreiben. Wie so viele unter den Komponisten dieser bewegten, aber kühnen Periode fand Arne die englische Musik im Übergangsstadium von der bestehenden Händelschen Manier zu dem leichteren, vom "Affekt" bestimmten Stil der frühklassischen Komponisten; die Suite wich der Sonate, Menuetten und Gavotten wurde der Vorzug vor Präludien und Fugen gegeben.

Arnes Laufbahn vollzog sich hauptsächlich auf dem Gebiet des Theaters, wo seine melodischen Gaben nicht nur in der italianisierenden Oper, sondern auch in Maskenspiel und Pantomime seinen Erfolg sicherten. Seine Ernennung zum Komponisten der Vauxhall Gardens 1754 bedeutete, daß er zusätzlich zu Liedern auch Orgelkonzerte schreiben mußte, die ein Merkmal der Konzerte dort waren. Abgesehen davon umfaßte seine veröffentlichte konzertante Instrumentalmusik Orchesterouvertüren und eine Gruppe von sieben Triosonaten.

Daß Arne keine Voluntaries für Orgel hinterließ, mag dem Umstand zuzuschreiben sein, daß er (im Gegensatz zu vielen wohlbekannten musikalischen Zeitgenossen) Katholik war. Tatsächlich waren seine einzigen veröffentlichten Kompositionen für solistisches Tasteninstrument die Sonaten, die John Walsh für den 26. November 1756 im *Public Advertizer* ankündigte:

NEW MUSIC
This day is published, Price 6s.
EIGHT Sonatas or Lessons for the
Harpsicord, compos'd by Mr. Arne
(Neue Musik – *Heute erscheinen*, Preis 6 Schilling – Acht Sonaten oder Lektionen für das Cembalo, – komponiert von Herrn Arne.)

Die Sammlung trägt alle Anzeichen dafür hastig zusammengestellt worden zu sein. Es war ungewöhnlich, acht Sonaten (statt sechs oder zwölf) zusammenzugruppieren, und die Folge der Sätze und Tonarten ist in mehreren Sonaten besonders zufällig, was darauf schließen läßt, daß sie aufs Geratewohl aus einer Zahl von Sätzen zusammengetragen worden waren. An einigen Stellen hat Arne selbst eine kurze verbindende Passage vorgeschlagen, um einen ungeschickten Übergang auszugleichen (wie in der Sonate Nr. 1), an anderen Stellen bleibt dies dem Spieler überlassen (Sonaten Nr. 2 und Nr. 6).

Walsh zeigte auf Arnes originalem Titelblatt noch andere Komponisten an (Galuppi, Ciampi, Alberti, Pasquini, Bononcini usw.), woraus sich die englische Vorliebe für die italienische Art ohne weiteres folgern läßt. Unter den Engländern war Arne besonders kühn in der Übernahme von Neuerungen von Zipoli, Alberti und ganz

deutlich von Scarlatti. Er gehörte zu "mehreren Subskribenten" (zusammen mit Avison, Boyce, Pepusch, Stanley und Geminiani) der zweibändigen Sammlung von Scarlattis Sonaten, die 1739 erschien, und der Einfluß zeigt sich deutlich in den Allegro-Sätzen der Sonaten Nr. 1 und Nr. 3 und ebenso in den Schlußvariationen der Sonate Nr. 6. Die kürzere und nervösere Diktion des Anfangs von Sonate Nr. 2 hingegen spiegelt die "galante" Art der deutschen Komponisten wider, und das folgende Adagio (ein merkwürdig für sich stehender Satz, der einer Erklärung bedarf) kommt dem englischen Voluntary so nahe wie kein anderer Satz bei Arne.

Die Sonate Nr. 3 beginnt mit einem Präludium, dem Arne die Anweisung hinzufügt, daß "In diesem und in anderen Präludien, die als Extempore-Spiel vor dem eigentlichen Beginn der Lektion gemeint sind, weder der Komponist noch der Ausführende zur strikten Einhaltung des Taktes verpflichtet sind". Händel hatte mehrere solcher Präludien in seine erste Suitensammlung für Tasteninstrument hineingenommen, und die ganze Sonate insgesamt zielt mehr auf eine gewichtigere, barockere Wirkung als die vorangehenden zwei, mit genau festgelegten Solo- und Tutti-Abschnitten im zweiten Satz, die das Concerto grosso widerspiegeln.

Die längste und unausgewogenste Sonate (Nr. 4) liefert den deutlichsten Beweis für die Unvereinbarkeit der Bestandteile, die Arne für die Sammlung zusammenbrachte. Sowohl die großartige auftaktige Fuge (die einzige in der Sammlung) als auch die abschließende "Jigg" sind eindeutige Beispiele für den englischen Stil und absolut idiomatisch für das Tasteninstrument geschrieben. Das eröffnende Andante, ebenso idiomatisch, neigt mehr zur "expressiven" Art mit starkem Gebrauch von "Seufzer-Kadenzen" und einigen geschickt mit synkopierter Chromatik gedehnten Passagen; das Siciliano jedoch liegt so wenig gut für das Tasteninstrument, daß es eher als eine hastige Umarbeitung eines Satzes angesehen werden kann, der ursprünglich für ein Melodieinstrument mit beziffertem Baß bestimmt war.[1]

Arne selbst gestand in seiner Überschrift die Zufälligkeit in der Entstehung der Sonate Nr. 8 ein: "Das folgende schlichte Menuett ist nicht von Herrn Arne; sondern er komponierte (auf Ersuchen einer Dame) den Baß und die folgenden Variationen, um es zu einer ansprechenden Lektion für das Cembalo zu machen". Die selbe Melodie (mit geringfügigen Erweiterungen) wurde später von Tenducci als Arie in seinem Pasticcio *Athridates* (veröffentlicht von John Johnston 1767) entlehnt, wo sie zu den Worten "Where is pitty's melting Eye?" gesungen und "Mr. Rameau" zugeschrieben wurde.[2]

---

[1] Weitere Erörterungen der historischen Stellung von Arnes Sonaten in A. E. F. Dickinson, "Arne and the keyboard sonata", in: The Monthly Musical Record, Mai 1955, S. 88-95, und in William S. Newman, The Sonata in the Baroque Era, The University of North Carolina Press, 1959, S. 328-330.

[2] Die Auskunft wurde freundlicherweise von John A. Parkinson gegeben.

Da kein Autograph der Sonaten erhalten ist, basiert die vorliegende Ausgabe auf der Veröffentlichung von Walsh aus dem Jahr 1756 (Quelle **A** in den Editorial Notes); Folio Querformat, paginiert 2-32. Die Titelseite lautet: VIII / SONATAS / OR / LESSONS FOR THE HARPSICHORD / COMPOS'D BY / THOMAS AUGUSTINE ARNE./ [rule] / London. Printed for I. Walsh in Catharine Street in the Strand. / [extended advertisement]. (VIII / Sonaten / oder / Lektionen für das Cembalo / komponiert von / Thomas Augustine Arne. / [Linie] / London. Gedruckt für I. Walsh in der Catherine Street in the Strand. / [ausgedehnte Anzeige]).

Nach der Zahl der in europäischen und amerikanischen Sammlungen überlieferten Exemplare zu urteilen, könnte die Ausgabe wohl weit verbreitet gewesen sein, doch wurden die Sonaten nicht vor 1879 wieder veröffentlicht, als Ernst Pauer sie (mit wesentlichen redaktionellen Zusätzen) in seine kühne Publikation der *Old English Composers for the Virginals & Harpsichord* (London, Augener & Co.) aufnahm. 1969 kam ein "Faksimile der ersten Ausgabe" heraus (Stainer & Bell Ltd, London) nach einem Exemplar der Veröffentlichung von 1756, das damals Thurston Dart gehörte und heute in der Bibliothek des Music Department, King's College, Universität London aufbewahrt wird. Diese Faksimile-Vorlage ist leider in gewisser Weise "trügerisch". Eine geringe Zahl von Verbesserungen am Text (zumeist die Entfernung von Trillern der linken Hand) legt eine zweite Ausgabe der ersten Edition nahe, obgleich kein anderes Exemplar bisher bekannt geworden ist. Sie enthält überdies wesentliche handschriftliche Ergänzungen, der Schrift nach zu urteilen aus dem 18. Jahrhundert; sie umfassen Haltebögen, Bindebögen, "V.S."-Angaben für Wendestellen, Kustoden und eine (für das 18. Jahrhundert) erstaunliche Zahl von Warnungsakzidentien und überflüssigen Vorzeichen.[3] Die Tatsache, daß der Originaldruck (in seinen eigenen Worten) erstaunlich frei von Druckfehlern und Auslassungen war, spricht dagegen, daß die handschriftlichen Ergänzungen sich auf Versehen des Komponisten beziehen, und da keine Verbindung zu Arne hergestellt werden kann, sind Lesarten dieser Quelle als redaktionell gekennzeichnet oder in den Editorial notes als Quelle **B** aufgeführt.

Die vorliegende Ausgabe ist daher der erste moderne Druck, der den Text von 1756 wiedergibt. Redaktionelle Zusätze sind kenntlich gemacht durch den Gebrauch von eckigen Klammern [ ], Noten, Pausen und Akzidentien im Kleinstich und ⌒ . Eine einzige im Tenorschlüssel notierte Passage (Sonate Nr. 4, 3. Satz. T. 10-12) wurde modernisiert, die originalen Widersprüchlichkeiten in der Triolennotierung hingegen (z.B. in Sonate Nr. 2 fast niemals mit Bindebogen und in Sonate Nr. 7 fast immer) wurden beibehalten. Hinweise auf die Verteilung auf rechte und linke Hand wurden übernommen, ebenso der bezifferte Baß für das Thema der Sonate Nr. 8 (der leicht im Zusammenhang mit den folgenden Variationen ausgeführt werden kann). Arnes kurze verbindende Kadenzen

und Arpeggio-Abschnitte (eine Grundlage für einfache improvisierte bravouröse Passagen) liefern knappe Muster, die die Spieler auch an anderen Stellen anwenden könnten (z.B. in den Sonaten Nr. 2 und Nr. 6).

Arnes Notation wirft wenige rhythmische Probleme auf; die Sonaten Nr. 4 und Nr. 7 bieten Beispiele für zusammengesetzte Metren, die in einfacher Form notiert sind und bei denen die Notenwerte an 6/8 bzw. 12/8 angepaßt werden müssen. Ähnlich sparsam und klar ist Arnes Gebrauch der Ornamente; *tr* und ᪸ (Triller und Mordent) sind seine einzigen Abbreviaturen. (Das einmalige Vorkommen von ᪸ in der Sonate Nr. 4, Satz 1, T. 25 ist offensichtlich ein Stichfehler für ᪸ .) Triller erfordern fast immer einen Nachschlag, ob er angegeben ist oder nicht, und beginnen grundsätzlich auf der oberen Note. Viele Komponisten um 1750 lassen jedoch auch kurze Triller mit Beginn auf der Hauptnote gelten, allerdings nur in bestimmten Zusammenhängen. J. C. Heck, Edward Miller und James Hook z.B. erklären sie als "nur bei absteigenden Noten gebraucht",

ausgeführt

(s. Sonate Nr. 2, Satz 3, und Sonate Nr. 7, Satz 3). Ein Vorschlag ♩♩ muß sehr oft mit einem Triller auf der zweiten Note gespielt werden und die Kadenzfigur ♩.♩♩ stets mit einem Triller auf der ersten Note. Der Vorschlag selbst (gewöhnlich, aber nicht immer von Arne mit dem halben Wert der Note notiert, zu der er gehört) "sollte ziemlich lang gespielt werden, wobei er mehr als die Hälfte der Länge oder Zeit der dazugehörigen Note erhält" (Geminiani, 1751). Ausnahmen, die als Vorschläge auf dem Schlag oder vor dem Schlag angesehen werden können, sind schnelle Passagen und Triolen-Figuren wie

C. Ph. E. Bach äußert dazu:

"Die Vorschläge vor den Triolen werden auch kurtz abgefertigt, damit die Natur der Triole deutlich bleibe . . . und widrigenfalls dieser Ausdruck mit dem ♪♩♩ nicht verwirret werde" [das Notenbeispiel wurde hier dem von Arne angepaßt].

Arnes Gebrauch von ♩♫♪ im Andante der Sonate Nr. 4 (der "empfindsamste" Satz der Sammlung) ist eindeutig eine Alternative zu C. Ph. E. Bachs ᪽ .

Ich danke folgenden Bibliotheken für ihre Mitwirkung bei der Vorbereitung dieser Ausgabe:

Universität London, King's College
British Library, Reference Division
Rowe Music Library, King's College, Cambridge
Royal College of Music
Universität London, Music Library
Reid Music Library der Universität Edinburgh.
Ferner danke ich Dr. Howard Ferguson für seine gewissenhafte Unterstützung.

---

[3] In der Faksimileausgabe sind diese Ergänzungen von dem gestochenen Text leider nicht zu unterscheiden.

© CHRISTOPHER HOGWOOD
Cambridge 1982

Übersetzung: Ruth Blume

vii

INTRODUCTION

John Stafford Smith, qui connaissait bien Arne, l'a une fois dépeint comme "un papiste vaniteux, un homme aux moeurs dissolues, mais auquel Dieu a donné le génie de la mélodie"; et son talent lyrique compensait indubitablement ses débordements et ses faiblesses. Il naquit l'année où Haendel arriva en Angleterre (1710), et à sa mort, en 1778, Mozart avait déjà vingt-deux ans et allait écrire sa symphonie 'parisienne'. Comme tant de compositeurs de cette instable mais aventureuse période, Arne trouva la musique anglaise en pleine mutation entre la solide manière haendélienne et le style plus léger, plus "apprêté" des premiers classiques; la suite cédait le pas à la sonate; on préférait maintenant les menuets et les gavottes aux préludes et aux fugues.

La carrière d'Arne s'alimenta d'abord au théâtre, où ses dons mélodiques lui assurèrent le succès non seulement dans l'opéra à l'italienne mais aussi bien dans le *masque* et la pantomime. Sa nomination de 1754 comme compositeur à Vauxhall Gardens montre qu'outre les airs, il devait produire aussi des concertos pour orgue, qui étaient une caractéristique des programmes donnés là. A part cela, son oeuvre instrumentale publiée comporte des ouvertures pour orchestre et un recueil de sept sonates en trio.

Au contraire de nombre de ses contemporains dont la renommée se compare à la sienne, Arne, peut-être parce-qu'il était catholique, n'a pas laissé de *voluntaries* pour l'orgue. En fait, ses seules oeuvres publiées pour clavier solo sont les sonates annoncées par John Walsh dans le *Public Advertizer* pour le 26 novembre 1756:

NEW MUSIC
This day is published, Price 6s.
EIGHT Sonatas or Lessons for the
Harpsicord, compos'd by Mr. Arne
(Musique Nouvelle – *Il est publié ce jour*, au prix de 6 shillings – Huit Sonates ou leçons pour le clavecin, – composées par M. Arne.)

La série porte tous les signes d'un assemblage hâtif. On trouvait d'habitude six ou douze sonates dans un recueil plutôt que huit et, dans plusieurs des sonates, la succession au petit bonheur des mouvements et des tonalités suggère que l'ensemble a été réalisé à partir d'un certain nombre de mouvements pris au hasard. A certains endroits, Arne a lui-même suggéré un court raccord pour adoucir quelque transition abrupte (comme dans la sonate n° 1), mais à d'autres moments, c'est à l'interprète d'y pourvoir (sonates n° 2 et n° 6).

D'après les noms des autres compositeurs que la publicité de Walsh annonce sur la page de titre originale du recueil d'Arne (Galuppi, Ciampi, Alberti, Pasquini, Bononcini, etc.) on peut aisément déduire l'inclination des Anglais en faveur de l'italianisme. Arne était particulièrement aventureux, entre tous les Anglais, en suivant les innovations de Zipoli, Alberti et, très évidemment, Scarlatti. Il fut l'un des "différents souscripteurs" (en compagnie d'Avison, Boyce, Pepusch, Stanley et Geminiani) du recueil en deux volumes des sonates de Scarlatti publiées en 1739, dont l'influence se manifeste dans les Allegros des sonates n° 1 et n° 3, aussi bien que dans la variation finale de la sonate n° 6. Cependant, les phrases plus nerveuses et plus courtes du début de la sonate n° 2 reflètent la manière "galante" des musiciens germaniques, et l'Adagio qui suit (un mouvement curieusement à part qui mérite quelqu'explication), est ce qu'Arne a jamais écrit de plus proche du *voluntary* anglais.

La sonate n° 3 commence par un Prélude, auquel Arne adjoint l'indication que "Dans ce Prélude et dans les autres, qui sont compris comme des esquisses improvisées avant le début de la leçon, ni le compositeur, ni l'interprète ne sont obligés d'observer un tempo rigoureux". Haendel avait inclus plusieurs préludes de cette sorte dans la première série de ses suites pour clavier, et l'ensemble de cette sonate vise à un effet de puissance plus baroque que les deux premières avec, dans le second mouvement, l'opposition tranchée "solo"-"tutti", qui rappelle le concerto grosso.

La sonate la plus longue et la plus disparate (n° 4) est celle où il est le plus évident qu'Arne a rassemblé des éléments hétérogènes pour compléter son recueil. Tant la fugue splendidement syncopée (la seule fugue de tout le recueil) que la "jigg" finale sont des exemples achevés du style anglais, écrits d'une façon parfaitement adéquate pour le clavier. L'Andante du début, tout aussi idiomatique, penche davantage vers la manière "expressive", avec son utilisation fréquente de la "cadence plaintive" et quelques passages chromatiques très habilement développés. La Sicilienne, cependant, vient si mal sous les doigts qu'on peut la tenir plutôt pour l'adaptation hâtive d'un mouvement avec basse chiffrée destiné d'abord à un instrument mélodique[1].

Arne a lui-même admis les origines fortuites de la sonate n° 8 dans sa présentation: "Le simple menuet suivant n'est pas de M. Arne; mais (à la requête d'une dame), il en a composé la basse, et les variations qui suivent de manière à en faire une agréable leçon de clavecin". La même mélodie, (avec de petites additions), fut plus tard empruntée par Tenducci pour une aria dans son *pastiche*, *Athridates* (publié par John Johnston en 1767), où elle était chantée sur les paroles "Where is pitty's melting Eye?" et attribuée à "M. Rameau"[2].

Comme aucun autographe des sonates ne subsiste, la présente édition se fonde sur l'édition de Walsh en 1756 (source **A** dans les Editorial notes), un in-folio oblong, paginé 2-32. La page de titre est ainsi rédigée: VIII / SONATAS / OR / LESSONS FOR THE HARPSICHORD / COMPOS'D BY / THOMAS AUGUSTINE ARNE. / [rule] / London. Printed for I. Walsh in Catharine Street in the Strand. / [extended advertisement] (VIII sonates / ou / leçons pour le clavecin / composées par / Thomas Augus-

---

[1] On peut trouver une discussion plus approfondie de l'histoire des sonates d'Arne dans: Dickinson, A. E. F., *Arne and the keyboard sonata*, dans: *The Monthly Musical Record*, mai 1955, pp. 88-95, et dans: Newman, William S., *The Sonata in the Baroque Era*, Chapel Hill, The University of North Carolina Press, 1959.

[2] Précision obligeamment fournie par John A. Parkinson.

tine Arne [trait d'union] / Londres. Imprimées pour I. Walsh à Catharine Street dans le Strand / [long avertissement].).

A en juger d'après le nombre des copies qui subsistent dans les collections européennes et américaines, cette publication paraît avoir été un succès populaire, mais les sonates n'ont été de nouveau publiées qu'en 1879, lorsqu'Ernest Pauer les a incluses (avec de substantiels ajouts de l'éditeur) dans son volume précurseur des *Old English Composers for the Virginals & Harpsichord* (London, Augener & Co). En 1969, un "facsimilé reproduisant la première édition" a été publié (Stainer & Bell Ltd, London), tiré d'une copie de la publication de 1756 qui appartenait alors à Thurston Dart, et qui est maintenant à la bibliothèque du Département de musique au King's College de l'Université de Londres. Malheureusement, cette copie est le type de l'exemplaire "farceur". Un petit nombre de variantes dans le texte (surtout la suppression des trilles de la main gauche) suggère qu'elle est une seconde publication de la première édition, bien qu'aucun autre exemplaire n'en ait été signalé. Elle contient aussi d'importantes additions manuscrites par une écriture qu'on dirait du XVIIIe siècle; elles consistent en notes liées, liaisons, initiales "V.S." pour tourner les pages, "instructions", et un nombre surprenant (pour le dix-huitième siècle) d'altérations redondantes ou de précaution.[3] Le fait que la publication originale soit (selon les termes-mêmes qui s'y trouvent) étonnamment épargnée par les fautes d'impression et les omissions s'oppose à ce que ces ajouts manuscrits soient des oublis du compositeur, et puisqu'un rapport avec Arne ne peut être assuré à ce propos, les leçons provenant de cette source sont traitées comme étant de l'éditeur, ou classées dans les Editorial notes comme source **B**.

La présente édition est donc la première publication moderne à reproduire le modèle de 1756. Les ajouts de l'éditeur sont indiqués entre crochets [], et par petites notes, soupirs, altérations et ⌒ . Un seul passage, noté en clé de ténor (sonate n° 4, 3e mouvement, mes. 10-12), a été modernisé, mais les inconséquences originales dans la notation des triolets (presque jamais notés avec une liaison dans la sonate n° 2, par exemple, alors qu'ils le sont presque toujours dans la sonate n° 7), ont été conservées. Les marques d'attribution à la main droite et à la main gauche ont été gardées, de même que la basse chiffrée donnée au thème de la sonate n° 8 (qu'on peut aisément réaliser à partir des variations qui suivent). Les courtes liaisons cadentielles et les sections en *arpèges* d'Arne (qui sont une base pour de simples improvisations ornées) offrent des modèles succincts dont les interprètes peuvent se servir en d'autres endroits, (dans les sonates n° 2 et n° 6 par exemple).

---

[3] Dans l'édition en fac-similé, on ne peut malheureusement distinguer ces ajouts de la musique initialement gravée.

La notation d'Arne pose peu de problèmes rythmiques; les sonates n° 4 et n° 7 offrent des exemples d'un mètre complexe noté d'une manière simple et les valeurs des notes peuvent les assimiler respectivement à un 6/8 et à un 12/8. Pareillement l'emploi qu'Arne fait des ornements est modéré et clair; *tr* et ✦ (trille et pincé) sont ses seules abréviations. (L'apparition, une seule fois, de ✦ à la mesure 25 du 1er mouvement de la sonate n° 4 est évidemment une erreur de gravure pour ✦). Les trilles requièrent presque toujours une conclusion, qu'elle soit notée ou non, et commencent en général sur la note la plus élevée. Cependant, beaucoup d'auteurs reconnaissent que des trilles courts, après 1750, peuvent commencer sur la note principale, mais seulement dans certains contextes. Des auteurs tels que J. C. Heck, Edward Miller et James Hook en donnent des exemples "utilisés seulement dans les traits descendants", par ex.:

joué:

(cf. le 3e mouvement de la sonate n° 2 et le 3e mouvement de la sonate n° 7). Une appogiature doit souvent être interprétée avec un trille sur la deuxième note, et la figure cadentielle invariablement avec un trille sur la première. L'appogiature elle-même (d'habitude mais pas à chaque fois notée par Arne comme ayant la moitié de la durée de la note à laquelle elle est attachée), "doit être assez allongée, prenant plus de la moitié de la longueur ou durée de la note à laquelle elle appartient" (Geminiani, 1751). Des exceptions, qu'on peut regarder comme des acciacaturas sur le temps ou avant le temps, comprennent des passages rapides et des triolets, tels que

où, suivant C. P. E. Bach, "l'appogiature doit être jouée vite, de façon que le rythme reste clair et sensible à partir de ". L'utilisation par Arne de dans l'Andante de la sonate n° 4 (la plus "empfindsam" du recueil) est évidemment une autre manière d'indiquer le ↯ de C. P. E. Bach.

Mes remerciements vont aux bibliothèques suivantes pour l'aide qu'elles m'ont apportée dans la préparation de cette édition:
Université de Londres, King's College
British Library, Reference Division
Rowe Music Library, King's College, Cambridge
Royal College of Music
Université de Londres, Music Library
Reid Music Library de l'Université d'Edinbourg
et je remercie le Dr. Howard Ferguson pour son concours scrupuleux.

Traduction: Pierre Bonniffet

SONATA I

Allegro

SONATA II

SONATA III

In this and other Preludes, which are meant as Extempore Touches before the Lesson begins, neither the Composer nor Performer are oblig'd to a Strictness of Time.

Prelude

Minuet

SONATA IV

SONATA V

Poco largo

Gavotta

SONATA VI

Sonata VII

Andante

Allegro

Sonata VIII

The following Plain Minuet is not Mr. Arne's; but (at the Request of a Lady) he Compos'd the Bass and Variations that follow, in Order to make it an agreeable Lesson for the Harpsichord.

EDITORIAL NOTES

The original pagination is indicated for each Sonata.

SONATA 1 [pp. 2-5]

Andante

bar 16	rh	grace note originally a quaver

Allegro

bar 17	rh n. 2	C
bar 34	lh n. 1	F
bar 63	rh n. 2	G♭ in **B** (MS alteration)
bar 14	lh beat 1	C quaver
bar 45	lh	D: no dot
		F: crotchet
bar 56	rh	trill originally on last note of bar 55

SONATA 2 [pp. 6-8]

Andante

bar 6	lh	last note and rest missing
bar 8	lh beat 3	F♯ and E♯ semiquavers
bar 9	lh beat 1	E♮ and D♯ semiquavers
	rh beat 2	originally [music: rest + semiquavers, tr]
bar 11	rh	♮ missing to appoggiatura

Adagio

bar 2	lh ⎱	G unmarked, even in **B** (although
bar 10	rh ⎰	G♯ is very possible)
bar 2	rh	crotchet appoggiatura
bar 9	rh	quaver appoggiatura

Allegrissimo

bar 48	rh	slur indicating 1st and 2nd time bars missing in **B**

SONATA 3 [pp. 9-13]

Prelude

bar 2	rh	original notation preserved, although [music notation] would more correctly be [music notation]

Allegro

bar 26	rh last note	C (MS addition) in **B**
bar 40	lh n. 5	originally a dotted quaver rest
bar 17	lh	the consecutive octaves are more visual than audible

Minuet

bar 20	rh	original notation [music notation]
bar 29	rh n. 2	G
bars 29 & 30	rh	the original notation of [music notation, tr] is preserved

SONATA 4 [pp. 14-19]

Andante

bar 4	lh beat 2	trill missing in **B**
bar 25	rh	ornament originally [music symbol] not [music symbol] as in bar 1
bar 34	rh	quaver appoggiatura
bar 35	rh	slur thus in original
bar 39	rh n. 1	ornament missing in **B**
bar 42 ⎫	lh beat 2	trill missing in **B**
bar 50 ⎭		
bar 66	rh & lh	superfluous dotted quaver rest

Fuga: Allegro

bar 10	lh beat 2	notated in tenor clef (until bar 12, beat 2)
bar 69	alto n. 2	G

Allegro 2/4

Conventional 18th-century notation for 6/8 throughout.

[music: 𝅗𝅥. = 𝅘𝅥 𝅘𝅥𝅮   𝅗𝅥 = 𝅘𝅥.   𝅘𝅥 = 𝅘𝅥.]

and all up-beats, whether quaver or semiquaver should be played

[music: rest rest 𝅘𝅥𝅮]

bars 18 & 19		originally notated as one bar, with lh B♭ a minim
bar 40	lh	second trill missing in **B**

SONATA 5 [pp. 20-21]

Poco largo

bar 3	rh	trill one note later
bar 15	rh	leger line missing to appoggiatura

Arne's original notation for a fermata is preserved in the cadenza linking the Poco largo and the Gavotta.

SONATA 6 [pp. 22-23]

Presto — all [music: rest] rests in the lh originally notated [music symbol]

SONATA 7 [pp. 24-28]

Andante — essentially in 12/8; [music: 𝅘𝅥 = 𝅘𝅥.] and [music: rest = rest]

bar 43		♮ missing to appoggiatura
bar 51		slurs indicating 1st and 2nd time bars are present in both **A** and **B** (though missing from the facsimile of **B**).

Allegro

bar 36		1st and 2nd time bars originally printed as one

SONATA 8 [pp. 29-32]

for the origins of the theme, see the Introduction; the original bass figuring is reproduced

bar 3	rh	appoggiatura lacks a tail. **B** suggests a crotchet, although a quaver would seem to be more consistent
bars 4, 12, 28	rh has D	all the remaining variations (and Tenducci's version) have F♯, and the theme has been adapted accordingly
bar 23	rh	appoggiatura B
bar 113	rh n. 2	D